Preface:

Welcome to this collection of dreams, where reality and imagination intertwine to create a vivid and unique world. Dreams are often seen as mysterious, unexplainable occurrences that happen during our unconscious state, but they have the power to inspire, motivate, and offer guidance in our waking lives. Each dream in this book is a personal journey, a glimpse into the inner workings of the human mind and its limitless potential.

As you read these dreams, I invite you to reflect on your own experiences and the symbolism and messages they may hold. While the interpretation of dreams is subjective and varies from person to person, there is no denying the power they hold. May these dreams ignite your creativity and inspire you to delve deeper into the mysteries of your own subconscious mind.

Dreams are not just the stuff of sleep, but are a manifestation of our deepest desires, fears, and aspirations. They offer a glimpse into the vastness of the human mind and its potential for self-discovery and transformation. So, buckle up and prepare to embark on a journey through the metaphysical, where there are no limits, only endless possibilities.

Beyond the Veil of Sleep.

My Journey Through the Realm of Dreams.

Contents

1. Haircut

2022

1. Haircut

The Haircut

Shaving, swirling drama, my clipper's

Handed to a random guy.

Asking unanswerable questions.

Leading me to a barber A wonky chair, a wonky wife

He returns from a run. Wife sits on my shoulders.

Hair cut unfinished. Dream unfinished. Morning.

Dream Interpretation

The dream may represent feelings of uncertainty or lack of control in some aspect of John's life. The act of shaving or getting a haircut may symbolize a desire to change or refresh one's appearance or identity. The presence of an unknown man and unanswerable questions may suggest feelings of confusion or anxiety about the future. The wonky chair and wife on the shoulders may indicate a feeling of burden or discomfort in making important decisions. The dream's unfinished nature may suggest unresolved feelings or ongoing issues that require attention.

2. Sumo

2022

2. Sumo

Sumo, Sumo, where are you?

Hunting, hollering through hours of terrain.

Loop back, looking down. Shape. Shine. Silhouette.

Shadow. Smell. Speed. Hear a sound.

Sumo found. Not seen in this dream!

Dream Interpretation

Based on the symbols present in the dream, it seems to suggest that John is on a quest to search for something or someone. The hunting and hollering signify the effort being put into this search, which requires traversing through unknown terrain. Looping back and looking down may represent a need to retrace steps or review past actions. The appearance of shape, shine, shadow, and silhouette may be indicating that the object of this search is taking form and becoming clearer. The smell could be associated with an emotional or intuitive sense that the dreamer is getting closer to his goal. Speed may represent urgency or the desire to reach the destination quickly. The sound heard in the dream could hold further significance, perhaps hinting at the identity of what John is searching for. The mention of Sumo found could indicate success in the quest, but the absence of this character in the dream leaves the actual outcome open to interpretation.

3.Suspicious Dreams
2022

3. Suspicious Dreams

Suspicious dreams, suspicious mind. Ulterior motives swim unconsciously. Conscious sights, sounds swirl into dreams. Chase starts downwards, spiraling into falseness. Fortuitous associations, journeys without endings. Jealousy, fear, anger surprise. It's not real, it's a dream.

Dream Interpretation

John may be feeling suspicious or paranoid in his waking life, as indicated by the phrase "suspicious mind." The dream may be exploring themes of hidden agendas or ulterior motives ("ulterior motives swim unconsciously"). He may also feel like reality and his imagination are blending ("conscious sights, sounds swirl into dreams"). The chase downwards and spiral may represent a descent into falsehood or deceit ("chase starts downwards, spiraling into falseness"). John may have experienced positive or serendipitous events recently, but they have not led to a clear destination ("fortuitous associations, journeys without endings"). The dream may also be exploring emotions such as jealousy, fear, and anger that may have surprised him. Lastly, he may be aware that this is a dream and not reality ("It's not real, it's a dream").

4. Never ending

2022

4. Never ending

Dreams that never end. Chasing, searching, moving. Be it a woman an enemy or friend. I never escape I never find or solve the dream. In and out of sleep, I'm awake it's a dream. Back asleep still in the chase, still running, still searching. With my eyes never seeing Proof of identity never obtained Deception, deceitfulness, doubts, nebulousness. Falling into the abyss never reaching the bottom.

Dream Interpretation

Based on the symbols and themes presented in the dream, it seems to suggest a feeling of being trapped in a never-ending cycle of chasing and searching for something or someone, but never being able to find or solve it. The dream also includes feelings of confusion and insecurity, as evidenced by the themes of deception, deceitfulness, and nebulousness. The abyss that you fall into represents the feeling of being lost and never reaching a resolution. Overall, this dream may suggest a sense of feeling stuck or unable to move forward in some aspect of his life.

5. Cheating

2022

5. Cheating

Cheating, Swindling women, girlfriends' lovers. Never caught in the act. Mates talking scheming, plotting. Never caught in the dream. Never a happy ending, never a pleasant ending. The dreams continue nightly Exhausting physical journeys.

Dream Interpretation

The recurring dream of cheating and swindling women suggests that John may have feelings of guilt or remorse towards their past actions in regard to romantic relationships. He may feel that he has wronged someone and has not yet been caught or brought to justice. The involvement of John's friends plotting and scheming may indicate a lack of trust or betrayal within their close relationships. The fact that he is never caught in the act suggests a fear of punishment or consequences for his actions. The theme of never having a happy or pleasant ending may indicate a sense of hopelessness or negativity in John's outlook on his situation. The exhausting physical journeys in the dream may signify the emotional toll that these feelings and experiences are taking on him. Overall, the dream may be reflecting John's need to address and resolve past relationship issues and find a sense of peace and closure.

6. No Dream

2022

6. No Dream

No Dream night. Nothing dead space. Fractured images split into sleep.

Work, travel, home. No revelations, no experiences.

You cannot make up a dream. Dreams scream. Dreams are serene.

Dream Interpretation

It appears that John has been experiencing fractured and disconnected dreams which lack any clear themes or symbols. He may feel like he is going through the motions in his waking life with little excitement or inspiration. The mention of "nothing dead space" suggests a desire for constant stimulation and activity. The contrasting statements about dreams screaming and being serene may indicate inner conflict or confusion within himself. Overall, this dream description portrays a sense of detachment and restlessness in John's state of mind.

7. Divers

2022

7. Divers

Leaving surface. Wearing a KMB 18.

Surface supplied gas. No Bail out, weights, naked!

Task glowered from depth. Shimmering skin glistens.

Beautiful bottom, surrounded by a glow. The only tool needed, an erection.

Erection wakes me from the dream. Job not completed, on surface.

Dream Interpretation

This dream is related to diving or some type of underwater activity. The KMB 18 may represent a specific type of diving equipment or apparatus. The mention of surface supplied gas suggests a need for a lifeline or constant source of air while diving. The lack of bail out and weights may indicate a feeling of vulnerability or lack of control in this situation. Being naked could also symbolize vulnerability or exposure.

The task that glowered from depth suggests that there is a challenging or difficult objective to be accomplished in this dive. The shimmering skin and beautiful bottom surrounded by a glow could represent a sense of wonder or awe at the underwater environment.

The Erection that wakes him from the dream may symbolize a physical or emotional arousal, but it is unclear if this is related to the underwater activity or not. The job not being completed on the surface may suggest a sense of unfinished business or unresolved issues related to the dive.

Overall, the dream may indicate a desire for adventure, exploration, or a sense of pushing oneself to complete a challenging task or goal. However, it may also suggest a need for caution or preparation, as there are potential risks and challenges associated with this type of activity.

8.Lost Password

2022

8. Lost Password

Password nightmare. Username, given at birth. Cannot change Username.

First Password decided for you. Lost your password?

Change your password? You cannot swap your password to that!

No such religion. You have had 3 attempts your life is frozen. Open a new life, click here.

Dream Interpretation

The theme of technology and online communication is present in the dream, as seen by the references to usernames and passwords. The feeling of being trapped, unable to change or update one's username or password, suggests a sense of powerlessness or feeling trapped in a situation or identity. The reference to being unable to swap passwords to a particular religion could suggest feelings of religious or cultural exclusion or limitations. The idea of having three attempts before one's life is frozen could symbolize a fear of failure or the idea that one's mistakes or missteps have serious consequences. The final suggestion to "open a new life" could represent a desire or opportunity for a fresh start or new beginning in some aspect of the dreamer's life. Overall, this dream may be exploring feelings of limitation, powerlessness, and a desire for change or renewal in some aspect of John’s life.

9.Forbidden
fruit
2022

9. Forbidden fruit

Overgrown back garden. Misty morning dew. Hanging low, bunches, size of fists. Succulent blackberries. Vibrant raspberries. Scrumptious strawberries. Ready for picking. Cannot get close. Fading away. Into the darkness. Gone.

Dream Interpretation

The overgrown back garden in the dream may represent neglected or forgotten aspects of your life. The misty morning dew may signify a fresh start or new opportunity that you are not taking advantage of. The hanging low, fist-sized bunches of succulent blackberries may symbolize hidden rewards or pleasures that are within your reach. The vibrant raspberries and scrumptious strawberries may represent the sweetness and joy in your life. However, the inability to get close to the fruit and the fading away into darkness may suggest a fear of missing out or a sense of missed opportunities. The disappearing fruit may also represent the fleeting nature of happiness and the impermanence of life.

10.Checking out
2022

10. Checking out

Again, a long night. Almost herculean fight.

Attempting to scarper. Sign out, sally, sortie.

Relentlessly in pursuit. Perpetually, nay Endlessly.

Cast down the wrong road.

Unceasingly left in the place I desired to leave

Institution, Establishment, life.

Dream Interpretation

The dream may reflect a feeling of being trapped or struggling to escape from a difficult situation, represented by the imagery of a "herculean fight" and an attempt to "scarper" (i.e. run away). This could be related to something in your waking life that feels like a constant challenge or obstacle. The reference to "Sign out, sally, sortie" may suggest a desire for a fresh start or a new direction. "Sortie" is a military term for a sudden attack or charge, so it's possible that he feels a need to be more assertive or proactive in making changes. The idea of being "relentlessly in pursuit" and stuck "perpetually, nay endlessly" could indicate a sense of pressure or expectation from others, or perhaps from oneself. There may be a feeling of being unable to keep up or meet certain standards. The mention of being "cast down the wrong road" and "unceasingly left in the place I desired to leave" could suggest regret or frustration at not having made different choices or taken a different path in life. The specific words "institution" and "establishment" may point to a dissatisfaction with certain aspects of one's current environment or circumstances.

11.Monochromatic
Dream
2022

11. Monochromatic Dream

Colourless, toneless, eerie. A journey through the twilight. Searching for wears.

Across plains, down abysses, up highlands. Through babbling brooks. Crossing raging rivers.

So close, emerging from the sleep. Search over, naked, cold. Unresolved.

Dream Interpretation

It could be interpreted as his feelings are lost or disconnected from his emotions and sense of direction in life. The Colourless and toneless environment could represent a lack of vitality or passion. The journey through different terrains, including abysses and highlands, could symbolize the ups and downs of life's journey. The search for wears could represent the search for something valuable or meaningful in life. The babbling brooks and raging rivers could represent emotions and inner turmoil. John's proximity to waking up may suggest a desire for resolution or clarity. However, the dream ends with him feeling naked and cold, indicating a lack of comfort or security in life. Overall, this dream may suggest a need for John to address his feelings of uncertainty and find a sense of direction and purpose.

12.Dive
system
2022

12. Dive system

Construction barge. Diving system being loaded.

Message overheard "Dive Supervisors to Deck”.

Old Superintendent 'dead walks past' “Call me!”

“Superintendents are not 24 hours” A room with

‘Crusher’ He separates a poisonous salad.

He eats, leaves. I leave lost, searching Uni campus.

Dream Interpretation

The construction barge in the dream may symbolize progress or forward movement in life. The diving system being loaded suggests a focus on exploring deeper aspects of the self or a situation. Overhearing a message about Dive Supervisors to Deck could indicate a need to take charge and be a leader. The appearance of an old Superintendent who is dead and walks past suggests the need to let go of outdated ways of thinking or behaving. "Call me!" may signify a desire for communication or connection with others. "Superintendents are not 24 hours" could indicate limitations or boundaries with authority figures. The room with 'Crusher' may represent a place of transformation or change. The act of separating a poisonous salad may indicate the need to remove toxic elements from one's life. The fact that 'Crusher' eats and leaves may signify a lack of concern for the consequences of actions. Finally, feeling lost and searching the Uni campus may symbolize a need for direction or guidance in life.

13.Bubble Car

2022

13. Bubble Car

Searching, turning back. Towards the lights.

Car lights cast my shadow forward. Bubble cars passes.

Looking unstable. Crashes into a mound and tips over.

One man gets outs while one struggles in pain. "Sign your name here!" I sign in two places and walk on. What did I just sign?

Dream Interpretation

The dream may reflect John's search for direction or progress in life, possibly represented by the "lights" that are being approached. However, this pursuit appears to be hindered by an undetermined obstacle or instability. The car lights and the dreamer's shadow may suggest a need for clarity or reflection on one's own identity or motivations. The passing bubble car could symbolize a fleeting moment or a passing opportunity that may seem alluring but ultimately leads to a crash or disappointment. The crash and the man struggling in pain may represent the consequences or costs of taking risks, or the need to face the aftermath of one's decisions. The dreamer's signing of a document may indicate a sense of acquiescence or acceptance of some agreement or commitment that may have unforeseen consequences or obligations, as suggested by the question "what did I just sign?" Overall, the dream may speak to the need for caution, reflection, and awareness of one's motivations, actions, and consequences in pursuing one's goals.

14.No Dreams!
2022

14. No Dreams!

Night without dreams. A void, emptiness. No fantastically outrageous adventures. Unconscious sleep. Not one-story peep. Still Darkness devoid of fabrications. No inventions, creations. Futility.

Dream Interpretation

John's lack of dreams could represent a feeling of emptiness or a lack of excitement in his life. The void and still darkness may symbolize a sense of un-fulfillment or lack of purpose. The absence of inventions or creations could indicate a lack of creativity or inspiration in John's waking life. The futility present in the dream may suggest a feeling of hopelessness or an inability to accomplish goals.

15.Two
Women
2022

15. Two Women

Two warm, wonderfully comfortable women.

Sedentary, In front a bowl of fruit. Fruit unbruised, unblemished.

Apples turned, inspected. Pears scanned for decay. Oranges studied for mould. I'm attracted to only one woman.

Both alike, brownie, cream aura. Fruit turning. Left uneaten.

Dream Interpretation

The two women in the dream may represent comfort and nurturing. The fact that they are warm and comfortable suggests a feeling of security and contentment. The sedentary setting and presence of a bowl of fruit may indicate a sense of abundance and satisfaction. The inspection and scrutiny of the fruit may indicate a need for careful attention to detail and a desire for things to be in order. The attraction to only one of the women may suggest a preference for stability and consistency. The turning and uneaten fruit could symbolize a fear of wasting or missing out on opportunities. Overall, the dream may reflect a desire for consistency, order, and a sense of abundance and fulfillment.

16.Glass house
2022

16. Glass house

Stunned by the vista. Amazed by the smells filtering through. A glass encased room overlooking the ocean. Shine and brine. Powerful waves crashing below. I stand in awe. On only a glass floor. Breathing the ocean air. Taking my fair share. As I spiral into the gloom and darkness.

Dream Interpretation

John's awe and amazement at the vista, smells, and ocean in the dream may signify a sense of wonder, fascination, and curiosity about the world around him. The glass encased room symbolizes a transparent and vulnerable state, perhaps suggesting that he feels exposed or vulnerable in their waking life. The powerful waves crashing below may represent overwhelming emotions or challenges that he is currently facing, while the glass floor may suggest a feeling of insecurity or instability. Finally, John's descent into darkness could symbolize a fear of the unknown or a feeling of being lost or disconnected from his surroundings.

17.Cave
2022

17. Cave

Encased inside. Opening an ancient zipper. I sit
facing a man recognized. No name comes to mind
Opening the zipped parchment. Revealing.
Nothing! As the light in the wet cave dwindles.
Low light. My movements restrained with chain.
Water running down my back. Am I drowning?

Dream Interpretation

The dream could represent John’s search for something meaningful or valuable in his waking life. The ancient zipper and parchment could symbolize a hidden or buried treasure, while the lack of anything revealed suggests disappointment or frustration. The unfamiliarity of the man and inability to recall his name might indicate a sense of confusion or uncertainty about John's relationships or social connections. The wet cave and low light may represent a sense of isolation or unfamiliarity, while the chains and water could suggest feelings of restraint or being overwhelmed. The fear of drowning may symbolize John's fear of losing control or being consumed by his emotions. Overall, the dream may suggest a need for John to explore new opportunities and relationships, while confronting their fears and anxieties about the unknown.

18.Car
2022

18. Car

Dashboard lights glowing. Headlights showing the road. Accelerating, towards my destination. Pedal to the metal. Then nothing, no power, no movement. A computer monitors. Turn off, turn on, nothing. Lights moving up. Lights moving away. I'm standing still, just waiting for impact.

Dream Interpretation

It suggests that John is on a journey towards a certain destination, as seen in the description of accelerating towards one's destination. The dashboard lights and headlights symbolize John's awareness and focus on his journey. The sudden loss of power and movement implies a struggle or obstacle that he may encounter on his journey. The computer monitors and its failure to turn on suggest John's reliance on technology or external factors to continue his journey. The lights moving up and away may represent a feeling of being left behind or not being able to keep up with the pace of the journey. Overall, this dream may suggest that he is experiencing a sense of uncertainty or doubt about his ability to reach the destination and may feel overwhelmed or stuck in his journey.

19.Coins

2022

19. Coins

My old friend asked for a hand. Building in Thailand. Coins discovered. Go to the architect for plans. Bangkok towed by a super tanker. Water Skiing golf. Seven mates twisted together. Shenanigans. Scary climbs the hard way. Mates pass me using the stairs. Descending, deflated, defeated.

Dream Interpretation

Old friend asked for a hand, this could represent a desire to reconnect with someone from the past or a need for help from someone who is familiar to the dreamer. Building in Thailand - Buildings can symbolize the self, so this may represent growth, progress, or development in the dreamer's life or a desire for change. Thailand could symbolize a desire for exoticism or adventure. Coins discovered, Coins can symbolize wealth or abundance, but in a dream context, they may represent a newfound insight or realization regarding the dreamer's personal values or worth. Go to the architect for plans - This may represent the dreamer's desire for structure or direction when it comes to their goals or ambitions. They may need to seek guidance or advice from someone who has expertise in the area they want to pursue.

Bangkok towed by a super tanker, this image may represent a sense of being overwhelmed or feeling like external forces are controlling one's life. Bangkok could also symbolize a desire for travel and new experiences. Water skiing golf, this may be a combination of two activities that offer fun and excitement. However, it could also represent the dreamer's need to balance work and play or their desire for a more leisurely lifestyle. Seven mates twisted together - This could represent a sense of strong bonds or relationships with others. However, the twisting motion suggests potential conflicts or disagreements that may arise within the group. Shenanigans, this term often refers to playful, mischievous behavior, so this dream could represent a desire for more fun or spontaneity in one's life. Scary climbs the hard way - This may represent the dreamer's struggles or obstacles that they feel are daunting and intimidating. They may need to work hard and persevere to reach their goals. Mates pass me using the stairs - This could represent a sense of being left behind or feeling inadequate compared to others. The stairs may symbolize a path towards success, and seeing others pass by suggests that the dreamer feels they are missing opportunities or may need to work harder to keep up. Descending, deflated, defeated - This represents a sense of disappointment and defeat. The dreamer may feel discouraged or let down by their current circumstances, but they must remember that this feeling is temporary and will pass.

Lads

2022

20. Lads

Bunch of Lads partying. Come across the back yard into mine. Invading my space. Using my kit, being mouthy. Starting to get messy. Gun used on his face, making a mess.

Now leave, don't come back. No more Lads. Leave me in peace.

Dream Interpretation

This dream may represent a feeling of invasion of personal space or privacy. The bunch of lads partying may symbolize social or external pressure to conform or participate in activities that may not align with one's personal preferences or boundaries. The use of John's kit and his mouthiness suggest a lack of respect for John's belongings or personal space. The gun used on the lads may symbolize John's need to assert boundaries and protect himself from unwanted intrusions. The desire for the lads to leave and not come back may represent John's need for solitude and a sense of control over their environment.

Photo

2022

21. Photo

Wonky old house. Two people waiting to be photographed. One loved. One unknown. In position, perfect light. Click, click, click. Flash shoots out, video starts to record. Twenty thirty times, same, same. No shot taken. Disappearing scene. Dream ends with a scream.

Dream Interpretation

The wonky old house could symbolize instability or uncertainty in John's life. The two people waiting to be photographed may represent different aspects of the self, with one being a known and loved part and the other an unknown or unfamiliar part. The perfect light and positioning could symbolize John's desire for everything to be just right or for things to fall into place. The repeated clicking of the camera and the video recording could indicate an attempt to capture a moment or hold onto a memory. The fact that no shots were taken, and the scene disappeared could suggest John's frustration or disappointment with not being able to hold onto a certain moment or experience. The dream ending with a scream could represent fear, anxiety, or a release of pent-up emotions. Overall, the dream may reflect John's desire for stability and control, and the struggle to capture and hold onto important moments in life.

Dream
Chaser
2022

22. Dream chaser.

Searching, hoping to dream. Yes, here's one. Not close enough to catch. Snatch from the ethereal. Fractured snippets, faces from the day. Unrecognized, unnamed. Wraithlike visions. Otherworldly people. Not my people. Not dreamland. Real world.

Dream Interpretation

This dream may suggest that John is reaching for something that feels out of reach or unattainable. The "wraithlike" and "otherworldly" people could represent John's feelings of being disconnected or disconnected from his surroundings. The fractured snippets and unrecognized faces could symbolize a sense of confusion or lack of clarity in John's waking life. Lastly, the contrasting feelings of not belonging to dreamland, but also not belonging to the real world may indicate a sense of confusion or difficulty in finding a place where John feels he truly belongs.

Dogs

2022

23. Dogs

Hell of a 'list' on the vessel Port holes dogged off Paint dripping off an open dog Running downwards in the direction I needed to go. Passing old work mates on my way. Barge foreman, Dive Supervisor chatting. I fly past with a nod. Continuing down the slope. Hitting the stern with a wallop. Waking with a start.

Dream Interpretation

The vessel and port holes may symbolize a journey or voyage John is undertaking. The fact that the port holes are dogged off and there is paint dripping off an open dog suggests a sense of confinement or restriction, or perhaps a problem or obstacle John is encountering on his journey.

Running downwards in the direction John needed to go could represent a sense of urgency or determination to reach a goal, despite the obstacles in his way. Passing old workmates on the way may suggest a reflection on John's past or previous jobs, and potentially some feelings of nostalgia or regret.

The barge foreman and Dive Supervisor chatting may represent authority or guidance figures in John's life, or perhaps a need for direction or support. Flying past them with a nod could indicate john feels confident and self-reliant.

Hitting the stern with a wallop and then waking with a start suggests an abrupt ending to the dream or a feeling of being jolted awake. It's unclear what this could mean in the context of the dream, but it could signify a sense of uncertainty or unease about John's journey or goals.

Dreamless
2022

24. Dreamless.

Nothing, not a flicker. 02:00 until 05:30. Not a single frame. Not a single fragment of imagination. A blank mind, exhausted. Unconscious stupor. Hotel bed, hotel room. Foreign country, different time zone. Praying for dreams tonight.

Dream Interpretation

It appears that John experienced a period of sleep during which he did not have any dreams or even a single thought. John was likely fatigued and in an unfamiliar environment due to being in a foreign country and in a different time zone. The reference to praying for dreams suggests that he may have desired to have a more restful, fulfilling sleep experience.

Gatherings

2022

25. Gatherings.

Twilight imaginations, not dreams. Reflections of Christmas eve. Gatherings of the clan. Regression while dreams flood back. Sister morphed from her now, to then. Crawling across the room on all fours. Disappearing. Clans disperse, memories fading fast. Days don't last.

Dream Interpretation

The dream may represent John's nostalgia for happy memories from childhood, particularly during holiday gatherings with family. The regression may indicate a desire to return to simpler times, while the sister's transformation may symbolize a yearning for the past or a feeling of disconnect from current relationships. Crawling on all fours and disappearing can represent feelings of vulnerability or a desire to hide from reality. The fading memories suggest a fear of losing the cherished memories of childhood. The mention of time passing quickly may indicate a sense of urgency to hold onto those memories or to create new ones.

Soliloquay

2022

26. Soliloquy.

Day at the races. Struggle to get the first bet on. The horse won by a length. We won the horse! Strips of flesh from its hind quarter. Into a Petri dish. Full of chemicals. LSD reacted to the horse flesh. Psychedelic experience. Changed the way I sensed the world.

Dream Interpretation

The dream seems to reflect a desire for excitement and a rush of adrenaline, as represented by the day at the races and the struggle to place the first bet. The victory of the "we" indicates a sense of teamwork and shared success. However, the unnerving image of strips of flesh being removed from the horse's hind quarter could suggest a sense of violence or exploitation. The Petri dish and chemicals may symbolize experimentation and manipulation, and the use of LSD to react to the horse flesh could represent a willingness to explore altered states of consciousness. The psychedelic experience resulting from this experiment may represent a transformative or mind-expanding experience, which changed the way John perceived the world. Overall, the dream may reflect a desire for excitement, experimentation, and exploration, but also raises questions about the ethics of using animals for entertainment and the potential consequences of chemical experimentation.

Faceless
2022

27. Faceless

Beneath the rookery stood faceless beings Gathering beside the babbling brook Stood, mingling, waiting for what? Me, maybe. The rooks started cawing while circling above No shadows cast from the group. No voices heard Unrecognized but known Fading into the mist of valley night.

Dream Interpretation

According to common dream symbols, faceless beings may represent a feeling of being disconnected or uninvolved with certain people in John's life. The babbling brook may represent a peaceful and calming influence in his life, while the gathering nearby could suggest a desire for social interaction. The presence of the rookery may symbolize death or foreboding, and the cawing may represent a sense of impending danger or doom. Additionally, the lack of shadows or voices could suggest a feeling of emptiness or loneliness. Overall, the dream may reveal a sense of uncertainty about the future and a feeling of being adrift or disconnected from others.

Perfect

2022

28. Perfect

Red hair cascading over perfect breasts pointing towards the holy grail. The same routine begins, caressing, licking, sucking. Sequenced, time and time again. It's all over too quickly. "Don't worry gets better with time" But it never gets any better, the dream always ends this way.

Dream Interpretation

Dreams often reflect our deepest desires, fears, and emotions. Consider reflecting on your personal experiences and feelings to make sense of this dream's imagery and themes.

Lost

2023

29. Lost

Searching for a landmass. Recognising features, attempting to locate position. Close then Lost again. Flitting from one zone in Paris. To the mountains of the Pyrenees. Frantic to find what? Lost into mountain mist, I disappear.

Dream Interpretation

The dream may relate to John's search for direction and purpose in life. The landmass and features may symbolize John's environment and the people and situations in his life. However, the struggle to locate his position and constant flitting suggest John is unsure of where they fit in and which path to take. The fixation on finding something suggests a desire for clarity or understanding. The Pyrenees Mountains may symbolize a hurdle or challenge that John must overcome. The disappearance into the mountain mist may symbolize feeling lost or uncertain about his goals and direction. Overall, the dream suggests a need for John to find his way and gain clarity about his purpose in life.

Chopper

2023

30. Chopper

Chopper, ditching into the sea. Down we go, kit and bodies. Follow the bubbles to the surface. Swim for land, escape and evade. Made it home, open the door. "Shush, I'm alive! we will claim I'm dead" I tell my first wife in a hushed voice. Again and again, I have this dream.

Dream Interpretation

John may be experiencing feelings of danger or risk in his waking life. The chopper crashing into the sea represents a loss or failure, potentially related to work or personal endeavors. The act of swimming for land symbolizes a desire for escape or avoidance of a difficult situation. John's survival and subsequent hiding of his identity from his first wife suggests a fear of judgment or reprisal from others. The recurring nature of the dream may indicate unresolved feelings or anxieties that need to be addressed.

Flirtation

2023

31. Flirtation

Fundamental flirtation founded on fun. Coquetry, collaborating, cajoling capers. Dancing a symphony, a cacophony of word innuendos. A minefield, tread carefully, take small steps, wait for the click. Boom, too late, one step too far. I got mud on my face. Now a disgrace.

Dream Interpretation

The dream may suggest that John is engaging in playful and lighthearted flirtation with others, enjoying the process of collaborating and charming those around him. There's also a hint of wordplay and innuendo present, possibly indicating a desire for deeper connection or intellectual stimulation in their relationships.

However, the dream also includes a sense of danger or caution. The metaphor of a minefield suggests that John is aware his actions could have consequences or risks, and he needs to tread carefully to avoid making a mistake. Unfortunately, despite his efforts, John may end up taking a misstep and facing consequences, hence the mud on their face and feeling disgrace.

Overall, the dream may suggest that John is navigating a delicate balance between playful fun and deeper emotional connections but is also aware that there are risks involved and a need to be mindful of his actions to avoid potential harm.

Inheritance
2023

32. Inheritance

"I'm giving this to Charlie" Why? "Because he is the first-born Son" "If I leave it any longer the brothers will get it all."

Grandad did not think this Inheritance issue through Bill has this and Bob has that. You get nothing. At least I leave something. No!

Dream Interpretation

The dream may be reflecting feelings of unfairness or resentment regarding inheritance or distribution of assets. The mention of the first-born son and the fear of the brothers getting everything may suggest a traditional or cultural emphasis on primogeniture or inheritance laws. The grandfather's lack of foresight may symbolize a lack of fairness or planning in familial or financial matters. The mention of Bill having something and Bob having something may represent a sense of comparison or competition within the family dynamic. The dreamer's final statement of "No!" may indicate a sense of frustration or disappointment in the current situation.

No!

2023

33. No

No! It's confusing, faces change, names change.
Locations change along with time. Time drags or time
flies. Danger comes to nothing. Pleasure turns to pain.
Happiness to sadness. Fear to comfort.

Dream Interpretation

John may be experiencing feelings of confusion and instability in his waking life. The changing faces, names, and locations in the dreams could symbolize a lack of a solid identity or a sense of rootedness. The fluctuation of time could represent a feeling of inconsistency or unpredictability in John's life. The fact that danger often comes to nothing may suggest that John is able to overcome obstacles or potential threats, although pleasure may turn to pain and happiness to sadness, indicating that he may feel like his positive experiences don't last. The presence of fear turning to comfort could suggest that John has a strong support system that helps him overcome his fears.

Beard

2023

34. Beard

Face with a beard Talking face appears up close and personal. Lawyer, solicitor, man of the law. Spouting off about family obligations. Responsibilities and commitments. Go away beard face, leave me alone. None of your business. Stow your bureaucracy. It's a family discussion. Keep out of our business. Gone, into the ether.

Dream Interpretation

The dream could represent feelings of being constructed by societal or familial expectations, particularly regarding responsibilities and commitments. The bearded face could symbolize a figure of authority or masculinity, and the fact that it is spouting off about family obligations may suggest a perceived pressure to meet familial expectations. John's desire for the face to leave him alone and to keep out of his business indicates a desire for autonomy and freedom from external pressures. The disappearance of the face at the end of the dream could represent a sense of relief or release from these perceived obligations.

White Stool
2023

35. White stool

White stool left as a warning.

Abusive phone calls. Angry face remonstrating. Spitting with anger as I stand my ground. Face to face he backs down. I now have the upper ground. As he backs away. Disappears into the gloom.

Dream Interpretation

The presence of a white stool in the dream may indicate purity or cleanliness, but in this context, it seems to have a negative connotation as it is left as a warning. Abusive phone calls may represent feelings of being attacked or bullied by someone in waking life. The angry face remonstrating and spitting with anger may suggest that the dreamer is feeling frustrated and angry about the situation. The fact that the dreamer stands their ground, and the other person backs down could indicate that the dreamer is gaining control over the situation or is standing up for themselves. The other person disappearing into the gloom may symbolize a fear of the unknown or uncertainty about the future. Overall, the dream may suggest that John is in a situation where he feels attacked or bullied but is starting to take control of the situation and assert himself.

Pizza

2023

36. Pizza

Don't recall a specific issue. Pizza keep coming to the table. No, take it away. A fracas ensues. Mama Mia! angry gestures. Waiters threatening advances. Cut! me doing Pull-ups from wooden beams. Elbow joints hurt as the muscles rip from the bone. Never did get that pizza.

Dream Interpretation

This dream may suggest a conflict or inner struggle between temptation and discipline. The abundance of pizzas coming to the table could symbolize desires, pleasures, or indulgences that the dreamer might find difficult to resist or control. John's rejection of the pizza and the ensuing fracas could symbolize a sense of guilt, anxiety, or pressure caused by societal norms or personal values. Mama Mia and angry gestures may represent the emotional intensity and frustration involved in this inner conflict. Waiters' threatening advances may symbolize external or internal factors that exacerbate this situation. Finally, the image of John doing pull-ups from wooden beams and feeling pain in the elbow joints could reflect the determination, effort, and sacrifice required to achieve a personal goal or overcome a challenge. However, John may feel that despite his hard work, he never received the reward or satisfaction he expected.

House

2023

37. House

Phone rings out of the blue. A very seductive voice. "Mr. Alden a property has just come up." "It's a writer's home in lower Nuttall, 300,000." Why are they selling? "His books are not selling well." No thanks. I hang up, turn over and go back to sleep.

Dream Interpretation

This dream may indicate a sense of security and contentment in John's current situation. The sudden phone call and seductive voice could be symbolic of unexpected opportunities or temptations. The offer of a writer's home in lower Nuttall may represent creative expression or the pursuit of a passion. However, the fact that the writer's books are not selling well suggests that John may be cautious about taking risks or investing in something that may not have guaranteed success. Ultimately, John chooses to decline the offer and go back to sleep, indicating a desire for stability and comfort rather than taking a chance on something new.

Tactile

2023

38. Tactile

Striking the most sensual pose. The second wife lay bare. So close, I could smell her. Feel her very presence. Even touch her, in this very tactile dream.

Dream Interpretation

The dream revolves around sensuality and intimacy. The presence of a second wife could symbolize a desire for something new, exciting, or forbidden. The act of being able to touch and smell her suggests a deep longing for physical connection and a desire to fully experience pleasure. The dream may indicate a need to explore and indulge in one's sensuality or a dissatisfaction with one's current intimate relationship.

The Bet

2023

39. The bet

People around me had placed a bet. I set off running, searching. First a jog then, full pelt. Down lanes, through fields. Turn left, turn right? Turn right, and run up hill, my choice. Turn around, run the other way. Pitch black night, I run on. Running to place a bet. Why?

Dream Interpretation

The presence of people placing a bet suggests a desire for risk-taking and excitement in John's life. Running represents John's pursuit of this excitement, taking him on a journey through different settings and forcing him to make choices. The pitch-black night may indicate a fear of the unknown, but John continues to run towards his goal of placing a bet, suggesting determination and a desire for reward. Overall, the dream may reflect a need for adventure and a willingness to take risks in pursuit of what John wants.

Fragments

2023

40. Fragments

Images flicker like light off a dark sea. Fragmented tapestry, unconnected events. Reflecting off my inner, unconscious soul. Surface, during an almost painful show. Remembering the past. Released from the dark recesses of my mind. You call them dreams. I call it, mental torture.

Dream Interpretation

John may be experiencing fragmented and disconnected dreams. The dreams may be reflecting his inner thoughts and feelings, possibly bringing up memories from the past. John may feel like the dreams are mentally torturous. The imagery of flickering lights and a dark sea may represent uncertainty and instability in John's subconscious mind. John may benefit from exploring these feelings and memories in therapy or personal reflection exercises.

Baseball
2023

41. Baseball

Standing alone, holding baseball bat. The field of dreams. Words pitched, with speed. Miss a few, hit a few. They are cheered as they disappear. Booed as they are caught. Three misses, it's a strike out! I'm gone.

Dream Interpretation

John's inner strength and ability to face challenges are symbolized by the baseball bat. The field of dreams represents the goals and aspirations that the dreamer holds. The words pitched may represent opportunities or challenges that the dreamer is facing in their waking life. Missing and hitting some may suggest that the dreamer experiences both success and failure in their endeavors. The cheers and boos represent the dreamer's perception of external validation and criticism. The three misses symbolize a potential failure or setback. Finally, the dreamer's departure after the strikeout may suggest feelings of defeat or giving up on their goals.

Finding
Space
2023

42. Finding space

Finding space, inside my head. Need room, for this important kit. Move that and make room there. No, that's important too. Okay, move that! Cannot, its connected to this. What's less important than this? Nothing. It's all part of the system. Me!

Dream Interpretation

This dream could represent John's need for mental clarity or organization. The act of trying to find space inside his head indicates a desire to prioritize thoughts and ideas. John may feel overwhelmed or cluttered mentally and is attempting to make room for something important. The idea of a kit suggests that there is something he needs to prepare or be ready for. The inability to move certain things may represent obstacles or difficulties in achieving this goal. Ultimately, John may realize that everything in his mind is interconnected and equally important, including himself.

Office

2023

42. Office

People, barge into the office, early. I'm nowhere near ready. Unprepared my words are a fluster. I search for the list, furiously, tapping keys. Send them away to sort it themselves. They all take a 'Green tee-shirt!' They think they are free. Nothing is free on here. Only abuse.

Dream Interpretation

Feelings of being overwhelmed or unprepared in a work or professional setting. The arrival of unexpected or uninvited people into the office may represent a sense of intrusion or invasion of privacy. John's struggle to find a list and his words being in a fluster suggests a fear of appearing incompetent or unorganized in front of others. The theme of being unprepared and the urgency to sort things out may reflect John's personal or professional life. The mention of a green tee shirt may represent a desire for freedom or a sense of rebellion against the constraints of their current situation. Alternatively, green could symbolize growth and new beginnings. The mention of abuse may indicate feelings of mistreatment or exploitation in the workplace.

Pool Game

2023

43. Pool Game

Playing pool, onboard our vessel. Vessel pitching, & rolling, with big seas. Line up the shot, about to strike, the white ball. As the vessel is tossed. Balls, fly away to the Port side. Line up again, hit the white. miss the red. Balls, aimed at, but never hit!

Dream Interpretation

John playing pool on his vessel represents his ability to maintain balance and control in his daily life. The vessel pitching and rolling with big seas reflects the instability and unpredictability John may be experiencing in his waking life. The act of lining up the shot and about to strike the white ball represents John's readiness to act and make a decision, despite the challenges he may face. However, as the vessel is tossed, the balls fly away to the Port side, indicating that his efforts may be diverted or obstructed by external factors. John's miss on the red ball suggests that he may be missing opportunities or failing to achieve his goals due to the unstable conditions. The balls aimed at but never hit may represent John's persistent efforts in facing challenges, but the results may not always be satisfactory or achievable. Overall, this dream may suggest feelings of frustration and a need for John to find stability and balance in his life.

Gifts

2023

44. Gifts

Gifts or presents. Bags full of inanimate objects. Nautical theme running through all. Compass, Carabineer. Knife. All shiny and new. Non-living but stirring my emotions. Am I, giving or receiving?

Dream Interpretation

Dreaming of gifts or presents may represent a desire for recognition, appreciation, or feeling rewarded for one's efforts. The bags full of inanimate objects could symbolize a feeling of being overwhelmed with material possessions or responsibilities. The nautical theme running through all may suggest the dreamer's desire to explore or seek new adventures. The compass may represent finding direction in life, while the carabiner and knife could symbolize John's ability to tackle challenges and overcome obstacles. The fact that the objects are shiny and new may suggest a sense of excitement or anticipation. John's uncertainty about whether he is giving or receiving the gifts may indicate a sense of ambiguity or confusion about his role in the situation.

Lifts

2023

45. Lifts

Going up, stops at the wrong floor. get out, searching but lost. Waiting for hours. Lift arrives, full. Empty lift arrives, takes me down. Door opens, people crush in. Squashed inside, claustrophobic. A floor unknown, I escape. Lost and disorientated, searching for a way out.

Dream Interpretation

The dream may symbolize a feeling of being stuck or lost in life. Going up but stopping at the wrong floor may represent goals or aspirations that are not being properly realized or achieved. Searching but being lost may suggest a lack of direction or purpose. Waiting for hours and the lift arriving full may represent feelings of frustration or impatience in regard to progressing in life. Taking an empty lift down may symbolize a fear of failure or experiencing setbacks. The door opening and people crushing in may represent feeling overwhelmed or being forced into situations against one's will. Being squashed inside and feeling claustrophobic may signify a feeling of being trapped or suffocated in one's current circumstances. Escaping and searching for a way out may represent a desire to break free from constraints and find a new direction in life.

Covert

2023

46. Covert

Covert relationships. Hiding faces, moving in shadows. Recce first, planning, scheming. Times worked out in preparation. Rooms arranged, houses rented, hotels booked. It's a laborious affair. A guilty dream.

Dream Interpretation

The dream may suggest that John is engaging in secretive or illicit behaviors, such as having a covert relationship or engaging in activities that require hiding faces and moving in shadows. John may be taking careful steps towards his actions, such as conducting reconnaissance, planning, and scheming, and preparing in advance. The dream may also indicate that john feels guilty about these actions, as the planning and arrangements required appear laborious and indicate an awareness of wrongdoing.

From the deep
2023

47. From the deep

Ascending from the dark, murky, ocean floor. Looking upwards, towards the surface light. Following my bubbles, at the same speed. No faster, or I will have an embolism. Swimming like crazy, reaching for the surface. Im sinking, back down into the darkness. Light disappears.

Dream Interpretation

This dream may symbolize John's desire to rise above his unconscious or hidden emotions and desires towards the surface of consciousness. The ocean represents the deep, emotional, and unconscious aspects of John's psyche. The bubbles may symbolize John's sense of direction or guidance. John is warned not to move too quickly, perhaps alluding to the need for patience and caution when exploring these deeper aspects of his psyche. The sinking back down into darkness may indicate John's fear of these unconscious aspects or his inability to fully explore and confront them.

Snake

2023

48. Snake

Hot and humid night, lay together. Interlocked, sliding, slipping bodies intertwined. Hissing, spiting sounds, a snake constricts my breathing. Gone has the perfect 10, replaced by a Boa. Squeezing the life from me Taking my last breath.

Dream Interpretation

The hot and humid night, along with the interlocking and slipping bodies, may represent a deep connection or intimacy with someone. The presence of a snake constricting your breathing could symbolize feelings of suffocation or being stifled in this relationship. The change from a perfect 10 to a boa may indicate a loss of perfection or idealization in this relationship. The act of squeezing the life out of you and taking your last breath could suggest a fear of losing oneself or dying emotionally in this relationship.

Crowd

2023

49. Crowded

A very overcrowded dream. Faces from the past, faces unknown. Mingling, networking, me in the centre.

Talking in a language, unfamiliar to me. A jargon of gestures between faces. I need to leave but trapped. An ever-decreasing circle of faces zooms in. Then fades with fear.

Dream Interpretation

John may be feeling overwhelmed or suffocated by social pressures or obligations. The crowdedness of the dream may symbolize a lack of personal space or individuality. The faces from the past may represent unresolved issues or relationships. The unknown faces may symbolize uncertainty or anxiety about meeting new people or being in unfamiliar environments. John may feel like he is the center of attention or pressure, hence the networking, but also feel isolated due to the unfamiliar language and gestures being used. The feeling of being trapped and the decreasing circle of faces may indicate a fear of being suffocated or controlled by others. Overall, the dream may suggest a need for John to establish personal boundaries and find a balance between social obligations and individual needs.

Family

2023

50. Family

An unruly family gathering. Flickering imagers bickering. They come one at a time, into my view. Sister, Cousins, Son, Wife, all arguing. All telling me I'm wrong. Thick and fast, they flit past my eyes. Word trailing behind, find my ears. "Worthless" "useless" "old man".

Dream Interpretation

The symbol of an unruly family gathering in a dream can represent issues with family dynamics or unresolved problems within the family. The flickering imagery and bickering suggest a lack of clarity and coherence in communication. Each family member arguing and telling John they are wrong could signify feelings of being inferior or criticized by family members. The words "worthless," "useless," and "old man" suggest a lack of self-esteem or feeling devalued by others. Overall, this dream may indicate a need to address underlying family issues and work on improving self-confidence.

Demoted

2023

51. Demoted

I am awake, not in my bed, not in room. I lay on the main deck of a barge surrounded by bodies. Diver's stare and whisper. I've been demoted, down to the decks, back where I belong. A Diver once more. Why?

Dream Interpretation

This dream may represent a feeling of being out of place or disconnected from one's usual surroundings. The barge and bodies may symbolize a sense of being adrift or surrounded by the unknown or unfamiliar. The demotion to being a diver again may reflect a loss of status or position in waking life. The diver's stares and whispers may indicate feelings of judgment or scrutiny from others. Overall, the dream may reveal a sense of disorientation and a desire to regain a sense of control or direction in his life.

Nothing

2023

52. Nothing

Unconscious night, nothing. Void of activity, no creative thoughts. No images, no stories, no memories. Just like a black hole. The gravitational pull, not letting out light. Holding on to my dreams. Captives for another night. Must rest my soul. Travel kills dreams!

Dream Interpretation

John is experiencing a lack of creative inspiration and mental emptiness, as if his mind is in a state of void. The absence of any imagery, stories, or memories suggests a disconnect from their subconscious mind. The black hole symbolizes a deep and dark void that is holding onto John's dreams, suggesting that he may be feeling stuck or trapped in his current circumstances. John may feel the need to rest and rejuvenate His soul, possibly by taking a break from his normal routine. The last line, "Travel kills dreams!" can be interpreted in various ways, but it may suggest that John feels that his aspirations and dreams are being hindered by his current situation or lifestyle, and that he is not able to pursue them as freely as he would like.

Poll

2023

53. Poll

A poll, with three very concerning questions. Questions, flash across my mind. Answer, which statement is true of you. Long sentences, delving into my sexuality. I refuse to answer, try to delete. Milliseconds later the same questions appear. Scrolling across my mind. No!

Dream Interpretation

Dream suggests that John may be feeling anxious or uncomfortable about his personal boundaries and privacy. The questions that appear in the dream may represent a fear of being judged or violated in some way. John's refusal to answer and attempt to delete the questions could symbolize a desire to protect His personal information or maintain control over his own identity. This dream may be reflecting deeper fears or concerns about vulnerability, trust, and the potential risks involved in being open and honest with others.

Dead Body

2023

54. Dead body

Black water I'm groping along the dock floor. Cold hands in the mud feeling the way. Hand goes through a decomposed body. Shocked I panic, retract my hand swiftly. Shoot for the surface blindly. Never arriving.

Dream Interpretation

The presence of black water in the dream may symbolize uncertainty or fear of the unknown. Groping along the dock floor may represent a search for direction or guidance in life. Cold hands and mud suggest discomfort or discomforting feelings. The decomposed body may indicate a fear of death or decay. Retracting the hand swiftly shows a desire to avoid negative or unpleasant experiences. Shooting for the surface blindly may symbolize a hope for escape or finding a way out of a difficult situation. However, the impossibility of arriving at the surface may suggest feelings of hopelessness or helplessness. Overall, this dream may represent a sense of being lost, overwhelmed, or stuck in a difficult situation with no clear solution in sight.

Car women
2023

55. Car women

Beautiful women with an intense look. Lounging against a huge tree outside. Weather is cold and wintery. I talk to the car while watching a drama on TV. The women asking questions. Questions I cannot answer. She deteriorates slowly. Forlorn and abandoned I leave her by the road. "Drive on!"

Dream Interpretation

The dream may symbolize a sense of awe and admiration for feminine beauty and power. The tree may represent stability or rootedness, while the cold winter weather could suggest a sense of emotional numbness or detachment. The drama on TV may represent life events or challenges that John is experiencing, while talking to the car may suggest seeking an escape, as cars often symbolize personal power or freedom. The questions asked by the beautiful women may represent a desire for answers or clarity in John's waking life, while her slow deterioration may symbolize a growing sense of disillusionment or disappointment. John's decision to leave the woman by the road may suggest a need for John to let go of something or someone in their life, and the command to "Drive on!" could indicate a need for John to move forward or seek new opportunities.

Upsetting

2023

56. Upsetting

Annoyingly long-lost dreams manifesting. Resurfacing only in fragments. Changes are introduced, parts lost. Not crazy, watered-down versions spin. Self-Censored dreams. Boring, drab, normal, not me.

Dream Interpretation

John may be experiencing a sense of frustration related to his subconscious. The long-lost dreams resurfacing in fragments suggest that John may be experiencing a struggle to remember or access their deeply buried thoughts and emotions. The changes and lost parts may represent John's fear of losing important aspects of his identity or self. The watered-down versions may symbolize John's self-censorship, possibly due to societal or personal pressures. The boring, drab, and normal dreams may indicate that John is dissatisfied with their current state of being and yearns for a more exciting and fulfilling life. Overall, the dream suggests that John may need to confront his innermost thoughts and feelings to achieve a greater sense of self-awareness and satisfaction.

Underwater

2023

57. Underwater

A simple, rolling hitch onto the hook. Coming up on the crane. The load, lodged under a lip. Carry on coming up, I turn away! On surface I walk past the next Diver. Getting chest compressions, laying on a mattress. He will die, I meet the surveyor to discuss the failed project.

Dream Interpretation

This dream appears to involve a series of disconnected events and symbols. The crane and load could represent burdens or responsibilities that are being lifted or moved but become trapped or stuck. The diver may symbolize exploration or going deeper into something, but in this case is bypassed. The chest compressions and discussion of a failed project suggest a sense of failure or disappointment. Overall, this dream may be reflecting a sense of being overwhelmed or unable to move forward with important tasks or projects.

Book

2023

58. Book

A message on my computer from Tommy. A new book on Diving, buy now! Opening the handbook, it looks and feels good. Better than the USN one. I'm envious and jealous. It's not competing with mine, different. Well done, Tommy.

Dream Interpretation

Interpretation could be that John is possibly feeling envious or jealous of someone else's accomplishments or possessions. The message from Tommy and the desire to purchase the new diving handbook suggests a possible interest or passion in diving or exploration. The comparison made between the USN handbook and the new one could show a sense of wanting something better or being critical of their own knowledge or resources. Overall, this dream could indicate a desire for personal growth or success in a particular area, while also acknowledging the achievements of others.

GPMG

2023

59. GPMG

The General-Purpose Machine Gun. Hangs heavy around my neck. Elvis's lookalike, Captain of the vessel. Turns the GPMG upside down and tells me to wear it that way. Nobody tells me how to carry a GPMG. I don't care who you are!

Dream Interpretation

John may be feeling burdened by a responsibility or task represented by the General-Purpose Machine Gun. The presence of Elvis's lookalike as the captain of the vessel may indicate a sense of authority or leadership in their life. The instruction to wear the gun upside down could symbolize the need to approach this responsibility in a different way or perspective. John may feel defensive about his ability to handle the situation and unwilling to follow orders from others.

Face to face
2023

60. Face to face

Face to face meeting gets heated. Same face multiple meetings. Inches apart, breath warm. Shouts in surround sound. Flicker out flit back in, same eyes stating me down. Rooted to the spot, spit hitting my face. Same message, no, no, no. Fades in a rage, no.

Dream Interpretation

This dream seems to suggest a recurring conflict or argument that John is experiencing with someone. The repeated face in multiple meetings could represent a specific individual or a pattern of behavior that John is experiencing. The closeness of the faces and the heated nature of the encounter suggest that the argument is intense and emotional. The presence of shouting and spit may indicate that John feels attacked or belittled during these confrontations. The repeated message of "no" may suggest that John is struggling to communicate or is feeling unheard. The dream ends with a sudden rage, which may indicate that John feels frustrated or overwhelmed by the situation. Overall, this dream may be reflecting John's feelings of powerlessness or frustration in a difficult situation.

Dog

2023

61. Dog

Snarling dog sounds, come closer. White teeth showing. Slavering, from widened jaws. Eyes, wide open. Nowhere to run, I'm in a corner. Trapped, back to the wall. Coming in low for the attack. Raises, up to his full height. Feared, looking into the dark.

Dream Interpretation

This dream suggests that John may be feeling threatened or cornered in some aspect of his life. The snarling dog could represent a situation or person that is intimidating and aggressive. The white teeth showing and widened jaws indicate the intensity of the threat. John feeling trapped with nowhere to run and his back against the wall suggests he may feel powerless or vulnerable. The dog's low posture and then rising up could represent the suddenness of the threat and the escalation of danger. John's fear of looking into the dark may indicate his fear of the unknown or uncertainty about the situation. Overall, the dream suggests John may be experiencing a period of stress or anxiety due to a perceived threat.

Empty

2023

61. Empty

Clean but empty white bowl. Always empty, never full. Carried by two small hands. From the street into a house through the open door. Door close's shut, with a loud bang. The bowl shakes with a tremor. Hands hold still, waiting. Hunger continues.

Dream Interpretation

The image of a clean but empty white bowl in a dream often symbolizes a sense of emptiness, dissatisfaction, or lack of fulfillment in some aspect of John's life. The fact that the bowl is always empty and never full indicates a feeling of constant emptiness or unfulfilled desires. The two small hands carrying the bowl suggest a reliance on others for satisfaction or fulfillment. Bringing the bowl from the street into a house through an open door may point to a desire for security and shelter, but the loud bang of the door closing shut signals a sudden change or loss of security. The tremor that shakes the bowl may represent John's anxieties or fears about what may happen next. Despite the trembling, the hands hold still, indicating an element of control or resilience in the face of uncertainty. Finally, the hunger that continues suggests an ongoing need or longing for something that John has yet to find or attain.

Dragging

2023

62. Dragging

Dragging a large sticky backed banner. Walking through a very large country house. Taking care not to let the sticky banner collect any dust. While looking back I bump into a friend. She is perfect, not aged a day. Looking surprised at the sight of me, an old man!

Dream Interpretation

Dragging a large sticky backed banner may symbolize a burden or responsibility that feels sticky or difficult to get rid of. Walking through a very large country house may represent exploring and discovering new parts of oneself or one's life. Taking care not to let the sticky banner collect any dust may suggest John is trying to protect or preserve something important to him. Bumping into a friend who looks perfect and hasn't aged a day may indicate a desire for eternal youth or an idealized version of someone from the past. Their surprise at seeing John as an old man may reveal fears about aging or a sense of disconnect between the John's current self and a former version of himself.

India

2023

63. India

Climbing through thick jungle. A path leading towards a lake. A man berates me. Pointing to the path he shouts in Hindi. I climb, getting high, getting scared. Near the top, I get stuck. Lowered down, trussed up with vines. The man, boy, disappear beneath the lakes surface.

Dream Interpretation

Dreaming of climbing through a thick jungle may represent your desire for exploration or overcoming obstacles in your waking life. The path leading towards a lake may indicate a desire for a peaceful and serene environment. The man berating you may indicate feelings of guilt or shame about something in your waking life. Him shouting in Hindi may suggest a sense of unfamiliarity or foreignness in the situation. Climbing higher and getting scared may reflect feelings of uncertainty or anxiety about the unknown. Getting stuck near the top may indicate a fear of failure or being unable to reach your goals. Being lowered down and trussed up with vines may suggest feelings of entrapment or limitation. Finally, the disappearance of the man and boy beneath the lake's surface may indicate a fear of loss or an inability to let go of something in his life.

Medical

2023

64. Medical

"What medical are you taking this year?" "A Diving medical, why?" "Well, you are over sixty now!" "Why not give up diving and become, I don't know? gay candle stick maker!" "I'm still doing triathlon training, I'm fit!" "The doctor here is a prick; he may fail you!" Dark room.

Dream Interpretation

The symbol of a dark room may represent feelings of fear, confusion, or uncertainty. It may also suggest a need for introspection or a desire to confront one's fears and anxieties. John may benefit from exploring their emotions and trying to identify any sources of stress or negativity in his life.

River

2023

65. River

Which side of the river will the 'bin men' collect from? The far side is easy! far side it's harder to get back. Getting back over with the bin turns into a dangerous situation. Life threatening, scrambling along the water's edge. Head and bin above the riverbank. I Survive where am I.

Dream Interpretation

John may be feeling challenged in his daily life, as symbolized by the difficulty of crossing the river with the bin. The river may represent a barrier or obstacle that the dreamer is struggling to overcome.

The danger and life-threatening situation may represent the fear of failure or potential consequences of not being able to complete a task or overcome an obstacle. John may feel pressure to succeed and fear the potential repercussions of not meeting expectations.

The fact that John survives and is left wondering where he is may represent a feeling of uncertainty or confusion about the outcome of his efforts. John may feel unsure about the direction his life is heading or what the future holds.

Overall, this dream may be a reflection of John's current challenges and fears, as well as his desire to succeed and overcome obstacles.

Theatre

2023

66. Theatre

Which side of the theatre should I go? Searching for the way out. Crowd hassling and shouting abuse. Dark and light areas, light comes from candles. Shadow cast shows my hiding place. I'm found and hounded out. What have I done wrong?

Dream Interpretation

The dream may be reflecting John's struggle to find direction or a clear path in life. The search for the way out suggests John is facing some kind of dilemma or decision that is causing confusion and uncertainty. The dark and light areas indicate john's conflicting emotions or desires, with light representing clarity and hope. The crowd hassling and shouting abuse may symbolize john's feelings of pressure or criticism from others. The shadow cast showing the hiding place could represent John's fear of being discovered or exposed. Being hounded out suggests john may be avoiding responsibility or consequences for his actions. Overall, the dream may suggest John needs to confront his fears and take decisive action to navigate his current situation.

Fuel

2023

67. Fuel

Driving on savannah plains. Watching the fuel gauge drop. Get more fuel to survive. Passing fuel stations, not stopping it's too expensive. Justify paying over the top prices against death. Run out of fuel and be eaten by lions, vultures. Pay the price, swallow your pride.

Dream Interpretation

This dream may symbolize a sense of survival and the need to persevere through difficult circumstances. The savanna plains and driving on them may represent a sense of journey or progress in John's life. The dropping fuel gauge may suggest that John feels he is running out of resources or support. The fuel stations that John passes but does not stop at may represent missed opportunities or choices that were not taken. Justifying paying over the top prices against death may suggest a fear of loss or death that is driving John's decision-making. Running out of fuel and being eaten by lions or vultures may symbolize the consequences of not acting or not making the right choices. Finally, paying the price and swallowing pride may symbolize a sense of humility or acceptance of difficult circumstances.

Magazine

2023

68. Magazine

Our onboard magazine containing recent projects. I read about our subsea discoveries. Then start on a satirical piece written about me. Mocking, critical look at my shortcomings. I get angry and ban further publications. Then calm down and find the humour. Laugh and read on.

Dream Interpretation

John's subconscious mind may be reflecting his interest in recent subsea discoveries and reading materials related to it. However, the dream also indicates feelings of vulnerability and insecurity towards potential criticism or mocking of his personal shortcomings. john's initial reaction reflects a desire to control the situation and prevent any further negative attention. However, john is ultimately able to find humor in the situation and let go of his defensive response. This may suggest a need for John to address his insecurities and learn to cope with critical feedback in a more positive and constructive manner.

Dirt bike

2023

69. Dirt bikes

On Dirt bikes we ride hard through the mud. Attempting every route towards the top. Top of a muddy wet landscape. Every attempt ending in failure. For what seems like an eternity, we ride. Undeterred, one goal in mind. The top, what's there?

Dream Interpretation

This dream of riding dirt bikes through muddy terrain and attempting to reach the top likely symbolizes a pursuit of achievement or success. The mud may represent the challenges or obstacles encountered along the way, while the dirt bikes and riding may symbolize a determined and adventurous spirit. Repeated failures to reach the top could indicate frustration or setbacks in reaching one's goals, but the perseverance and focus on the ultimate destination suggest a determined mindset. The question at the end of the dream, asking "what's there?" may signify a desire for knowledge or discovery of what the ultimate goal or reward may be.

Scaffolding
2023

70. Scaffolding

Scaffolding erected from the basement. Towering upwards through the ceiling. Looking outside, it surrounds the chimneys. Branching off into a cavity, I squeeze in and climb sideward towards the garden. Outside climbing a steel tree, difficult to make safe holds. I fall and wake.

Dream Interpretation

The dream features a prominent symbol of scaffolding, which is a temporary support structure used in construction. The scaffolding is seen to be erected from the basement, indicating a need for support and stability in the dreamer's foundation or emotional state. The scaffolding is also described as towering upwards through the ceiling, suggesting a desire to reach higher or achieve greater goals in life.

John also sees the scaffolding surrounding chimneys, which could represent a need to release pent-up emotions or ideas. The fact that the scaffolding is branching off into a cavity, which John squeezes into and climbs towards the garden, could indicate a need to explore unconscious or hidden aspects of oneself to achieve personal growth.

John then finds themselves outside, climbing a steel tree that is difficult to make safe holds on. This could represent the challenges and obstacles encountered in the pursuit of their goals. John falls, suggesting a fear of failure or a feeling of instability in his pursuit. Overall, the dream may be interpreted as representing John's desire for support and stability in his personal and professional pursuits, as well as a need to explore and embrace hidden aspects of himself to achieve growth and success.

Waking

2023

71. Waking

Searching for a place to hang a painting frame. Every angle, every height all walls. Never turning the painting to see its composition. I wake up and its midday. Missed a dentist appointment. Not for me, for my son! I look at my wrist to see the time; I don't wear a watch.

Dream Interpretation

John's search for a place to hang a painting frame might represent a need to find a suitable outlet for his creative energy or a desire to express themselves artistically. The focus on every angle and height of the walls could symbolize a need for precision and attention to detail in this endeavor. The fact that they never see the composition of the painting could suggest a fear of failure or an uncertainty about what they want to create.

Waking up midday and realizing he missed a dentist appointment for his son could represent John's concern for his child's well-being or his sense of responsibility as a parent. Looking at his wrist to check the time may indicate a desire to be punctual and organized in his daily life.

Overall, this dream could suggest that John is seeking a way to express himself creatively while also fulfilling his obligations as a parent. He may need to find a balance between his personal desires and his family responsibilities.

Passenger

2023

72. Passenger

The car shook as she woke. Voice from the rear, I looked over my shoulder. Swerving towards the buildings. Once under control, decided to take her home. Not mine, the chicken factory. They would take care of her. The journey on rails and bridges. Through water, over mountains.

Dream Interpretation

The shaking car could represent instability or uncertainty in John's life. The presence of a voice from the rear could symbolize a part of themselves or their subconscious mind that they are not immediately aware of. Swerving towards buildings could indicate a sense of danger or a feeling of being overwhelmed. Taking John home may suggest a desire for security or comfort. The fact that it isn't John's own home, but a chicken factory, may represent feelings of being disconnected from his own sense of identity or purpose. The journey through rails and bridges may suggest a transitional phase in John's life, with water representing emotions and mountains representing obstacles or challenges. Overall, this dream may be reflecting John's subconscious feelings of uncertainty and a desire for stability and direction.

Pie

2023

73. Pie

Jane, clean this area its filthy. A knock at the door, it's the council leader with Pie on a plate. He sits, the dog and cat eat all the pie. A cat appears with another pie on a plate. Man said he left that piece outside his door upstairs. Cat gave the plate to the dog, who loved it!

Dream Interpretation

The presence of the council leader may represent a figure of authority or power in John's life. The pie on a plate could symbolize something desirable or rewarding. The presence of a dog and cat may represent different aspects of John's personality or personal relationships. The fact that they eat all the pie could suggest a sense of competition or scarcity. The appearance of a second pie on a plate could represent an opportunity for abundance or growth. The man saying, he left a piece outside his door could represent the idea of missed opportunities or unclaimed rewards. The cat giving the plate to the dog could symbolize a desire for cooperation or sharing. Overall, the dream may suggest a search for fulfillment and a desire for harmonious relationships.

Fridge

2023

74. Fridge

Open the fridge this morning and it full. Not my food! where are my blueberries? No strawberries, none of my morning shake ingredients. My routine totally ruined. I cannot do my press-ups with my fruit blend as fuel. Day ruined.

Dream Interpretation

The dream may suggest a feeling of frustration and disappointment with disrupted routines or plans. The full fridge may symbolize abundance or possibilities, but the absence of John's preferred food and morning shake ingredients could represent a sense of lack or unfulfilled expectations. The mention of press-ups and fruit blend as fuel may indicate a focus on health or fitness goals that require specific resources or habits. Overall, the dream may reflect a need for flexibility and adaptation in the face of unexpected changes or challenges.

Again

2023

75. Again

Not exciting, same dream. Always searching for a way Lost with the destination never found. Every turn meets new obstacles, new barriers. Time is always the issue, running out of time. I'm late, going to be late again.

Dream Interpretation

This dream may symbolize John's feeling of being lost or directionless in their waking life. The constant search for a way may represent a desire to find purpose or meaning. The obstacles and barriers that keep appearing may represent challenges or difficulties that John is facing. The theme of time running out may suggest a sense of urgency or pressure in the waking life. The recurring feeling of being late may represent a fear of missing out or not being able to keep up with responsibilities.

House

2023

76. House

No right of entry, I need access to the land beyond. I needed to obtain a way, to the land and the stripper. The two mixed into one dream all about admittance. Sex drive, I couldn't buy the house without road approach, but could gain entry into the stripper.

Dream Interpretation

The dream may be reflecting John's desire or need for access to something or somewhere, represented by the land beyond. The stripper may symbolize a temptation or desire that John wants to pursue but may not have the means to do so. John may feel frustrated about not being able to achieve his goals or access what he desires, as shown by the inability to buy the house without road approach. Overall, the dream could be hinting at John's inner conflicts or struggles to gain entry to something desirable or rewarding in his waking life.

Rabbit
2023

77. Rabbit

I stand holding a live rabbit by its back legs. A Guy tells me he felt 'Erotic' when he broke his rabbit neck. I slammed my furry friend into a tree, smashing it skull. I felt sad, I killed my rabbit.

Dream Interpretation

Holding a live rabbit by its back legs: Holding a rabbit can represent the dreamer's desire for emotional fulfillment, gentleness, or vulnerability. However, holding it by its back legs may suggest a lack of care or a feeling of having control over the rabbit's life.

Guy feeling 'erotic' when breaking his rabbit's neck: This can be a disturbing and violent image, suggesting a potential fetishization of death or power. However, it's important to note that dreams don't necessarily reflect reality, and this guy could be a symbol for a part of the dreamer's psyche or experiences. Slamming the furry friend into a tree, smashing its skull: This is a highly violent and aggressive action that could reflect the dreamer's unresolved anger or frustration towards someone or something. The fact that it's a furry friend could suggest a sense of betrayal or hurt inflicted by someone close or familiar. Feeling sad for killing the rabbit: This is a common feeling after committing violence or harm. It could reflect the dreamer's empathy or guilt towards a situation in their waking life or unconscious mind. Overall, these dreams could point towards a sense of power, violence, and vulnerability in the dreamer's psyche. It could be useful to explore any unresolved emotions or conflicts that could be contributing to these types of dreams.

Gas

2023

78. Gas

Gas build bloats my belly. Pressure relieved with a long 'carving' knife. Inserted into the expanding stomach. Gas escapes and my pain disappears. This surgical operation repeated through a long uncomfortable night's sleep.

Dream Interpretation

This dream appears to be a representation of physical discomfort or digestive issues. The gas built in the belly indicates an accumulation of air or indigestion. However, the "carving" knife used to relieve the pressure might suggest a violent or aggressive approach to the problem. The act of insertion and release of gas could symbolize the release of tension or pent-up emotions. Additionally, the repetition of the surgical operation throughout the night might signify a feeling of inability to find a permanent solution to the problem.

Follow

2023

79. Follow

I follow a guy who knows which way to go. We walk into a building, a corridor full of people, all busy rushing around. I walk out into the open. Crossing a ravine, still searching, it's not there. I turn around and re-cross the muddy river. Two girls laugh at me, Im lost again.

Dream Interpretation

John may be searching for guidance or direction in his life. The guy they follow could represent a role model or someone they look up to for guidance. The busy corridor full of people suggests a sense of chaos or feeling overwhelmed by their surroundings. Walking out into the open may symbolize a desire to be more open or exposed, possibly wanting to take risks. However, crossing the ravine and not finding what they are looking for may suggest an unsuccessful journey or feeling stuck in their current situation. The muddy river may represent obstacles or challenges that John must overcome to find his way. The two girls laughing at John may suggest feeling judged or embarrassed by others for not knowing where to go or feeling lost. Overall, the dream may be highlighting John's need for guidance and the challenges he may face in finding his path.

Meetings

2023

80. Meetings

Meetings, gatherings all night long. Office meeting, people moaning. Meeting ends up in Hooters with me paying the bill. Wedding reception, in Hooters people are not impressed. Once again I pay the bill. Not one happy face all night long.

Dream Interpretation

The recurring theme of meetings and gatherings suggests a need for social connection or collaboration. The moaning at the office meeting could indicate dissatisfaction or frustration with work. The wedding reception being held at Hooters, a place known for its sexualized atmosphere, could suggest unease or discomfort with traditional social or romantic norms. John paying the bill in both situations could signify a sense of obligation or responsibility in these social situations. The lack of happy faces may indicate a sense of disappointment or disapproval from those around John. Overall, the dream may reflect a desire for meaningful connections and a fear of social rejection.

Job

2023

81. Job

Bumming around the islands. Offered a place up north as the 'Dive master' come general 'Dogsbody'. I take out the 'Longtail' boat with the tourists onboard. This is paradise, but for no pay. What a dream!

Dream Interpretation

This dream suggests that John may be seeking a carefree lifestyle, symbolized by the image of "bumming around the islands." The offer of a position as a "Dive master" and "Dogs body," without pay, suggests a willingness to work hard and do whatever it takes to maintain this carefree lifestyle. The "Longtail" boat and tourists may represent a desire for adventure and exploration, as well as a desire to share this lifestyle with others. Overall, this dream may reflect a desire for fulfillment and happiness, even if it means sacrificing traditional career goals or financial stability.

Computer

2023

82. Computer

Me bragging about my Son's gaming computer. "Well it's got a so and so graphics card!" "The mother board is top of the range!" I built from scratch. They start asking about speed, lagging and bio's? "How did you change the DRAM speed?" I'm out of my depth, fade into the darkness.

Dream Interpretation

The dream suggests that John may tend to boast or show off about their accomplishments, particularly in regard to their son's gaming computer. However, the dream may signify that John may not have a complete understanding or expertise in the topic he is bragging about, as he becomes overwhelmed and feel out of his comfort zone when questioned further on the technical details. The dream may indicate a need for John to be humbler and honest about his knowledge and experience, and to avoid exaggeration or bluffing in the future.

Approval

2023

83. Approval

All eyes on each other as we mill around the waiting room. One at a time, called into an office and told, “Approved’ or not ‘Approved’. Who writes these appraisals? Do they know me! I get to write my own, how can it be less than ‘Approved’ Everyone glares at me as I walk away.

Dream Interpretation

John is in a waiting room where everyone's attention is on each other. They are called into an office one at a time to receive an appraisal that determines whether they are approved or not. John questions who is writing these appraisals and wonders if they know him. This may suggest feelings of insecurity or anxiety regarding how others perceive John, and a fear of not being accepted or approved by others. John's desire to write his own appraisal and ensure it is approved may indicate a need for control and autonomy in his life. The glares received from others may represent John's fear of judgment or rejection from others.

84. Festivals

I enter one after another, contestant request to join their festival. I agree because I cannot say 'No'. Bombarded with invites, I start to worry. My Movie is shit! My screenplay is rubbish! I start to tell the organisers and my dream ends in confusion and dismay. Imposter!

Dream Interpretation

The dream may reflect John's inner conflict about his competence and self-worth, as well as his tendency to comply with external pressure that may overwhelm him. The festival and the contestants may represent social or professional opportunities that John feels compelled to pursue or at least consider, despite doubts or reservations about his readiness or suitability. John's negative self-talk about his work may reflect a fear of inadequacy, criticism, or rejection that undermines his confidence and creativity. John's attempt to express their concerns to the organisers may suggest a need for validation or feedback, but also a fear of being exposed as a fraud or an impostor. John may benefit from examining his beliefs and expectations about success, failure, and authenticity, and finding ways to balance his own aspirations and limitations with the expectations and values of his environment.

Follow

2023

85. Follow

I follow a guy into an underground car park. Coming out on a steep rise into the daylight. The guy takes the ramp to my left, I go to the right. On the street I find myself in a quiz. "Name me a state, in India?" "Rajasthan," I answer with confidence and carry on with my journey.

Dream Interpretation

John follows a stranger into an underground car park, which could represent exploring unknown aspects of the psyche. Coming out into the daylight suggests a moment of clarity or newfound understanding after delving into the subconscious. The decision to take a different route from the stranger may represent a desire for independence or individuality. The quiz about Indian states may represent a challenge or test of knowledge, and the dreamer's confident answer may indicate a sense of self-assurance or competence. Overall, the dream could suggest a journey of self-discovery and a willingness to take on challenges with confidence.

Halal

2023

86. Halal

One restaurant has 'Halal' food served. The other has English cuisine, both have revolving doors as the entrance. Enter either and you receive a weapon to kill.

'Halal' weapon a spear, English a 7.62mm 'SLR'. Both look alike. Neither fit through the doors. Leave or kill and eat.

Dream Interpretation

This dream may symbolize a decision or conflict between two different cultural or personal belief systems. The two restaurants with revolving doors represent two paths or options, one with "Halal" food and a spear as a weapon, and the other with English cuisine and a 7.62mm "SLR" weapon. The fact that both options look alike may indicate that they are both equally tempting or desirable.

The weapons provided in each restaurant may represent the means to defend oneself or attack others, highlighting a sense of aggression or violence in the dream. The fact that neither weapon can fit through the doors may suggest that the dreamer cannot easily switch between the two options or cannot fully commit to either one without consequences.

The final choice of either leaving or killing and eating may symbolize the need to make a decisive action or choice between these two options. John may be facing a moral or ethical dilemma that requires him to either sacrifice something or take a risk to achieve his goals.

Social Media
women
2023

87. Social Media women

Two women, one from Facebook, one from Twitter. One curvaceous, the other a line drawing. Both sexually attractive in different ways. They start chatting while I sit and listen. What would happen if they saw me sleeping, dreaming about, them? Weird right!

Dream Interpretation

The presence of two women from social media platforms, one curvaceous and one in the form of a line drawing, may represent the dreamer's desire for connection with others in a virtual environment. The sexual attraction towards both women may suggest a need for physical and emotional fulfillment. The act of listening to the women chat while John sits implies a passive role in his interactions. John's concern about being caught dreaming about them may indicate a fear of vulnerability or rejection in pursuing these desires. Overall, the dream may reflect John's desire for meaningful connections and a need to explore his sexuality in a safe environment.

Cooks

2023

88. Food

New cooks onboard the vessel. I avoid the mess room; I avoid the other Divers. The complaints come thick and fast. "The food is shit,"." I can't eat that shit!" I eat it, tastes good, it's my fuel needed to drive me. Lobster, and steak in this dream

Dream Interpretation

The presence of new cooks aboard the vessel may symbolize a change or new beginning in John's life. Avoiding the mess room and other divers may suggest a desire for isolation or a need for space. The complaints about the food could represent John's insecurities or doubts about his abilities, while his enjoyment of the food could indicate self-assurance and self-acceptance. Lobster and steak may symbolize luxury, indulgence, or even success. Overall, this dream may suggest a period of change and uncertainty, but also a sense of satisfaction and self-sufficiency.

Bar Dive

2023

89. Bar dive

Drunkenly chatting as we queue for the bar. Inside it's a competition to see who can dive the deepest. No water, no equipment, but I win. Outside I give reversing directions to a white van. The van runs over a massive bunch of bananas, squashing the lot.

Dream Interpretation

Queuing for the bar and chatting drunkenly may reflect socializing and relaxing after a period of hard work or stress. However, the lack of focus and control associated with being drunk could suggest vulnerability to peer pressure, poor decision-making, or frustration. Queueing could also imply waiting for something or someone, anticipation, or feeling stuck in a routine or obligation. Diving is often associated with exploring the depths of the subconscious, facing fears or challenges, or seeking new perspectives or experiences. Winning the competition could symbolize a sense of achievement, confidence, or superiority compared to others, or feeling in control of one's feelings or thoughts. Not finding any water or equipment could indicate a lack of resources, preparation, or self-awareness, or being in a situation that requires improvisation or risk-taking. Alternatively, it could suggest a need to let go of external distractions or expectations and focus on one's own abilities or intuition. Giving reversing directions to a white van might reflect a sense of responsibility, helpfulness, or authority. However, the van running over a massive bunch of bananas and squashing them could indicate a lack of attention, coordination, or caution, resulting in a messy or wasteful outcome. Bananas could symbolize nourishment, health, or pleasure, or maybe a phallic symbol or a pun on "slipping on a banana peel."

Shower

2023

90. Shower

"Sumo, get in the shower you stink". Abject fear in those brown eyes as he gets in the cubicle. Sitting still while the fancy, expensive shampoo is applied. "There, not so bad, all finished." "Well done boy, now come on, I'll carry you down the stairs" "You heavy lump."

Dream Interpretation

The dream appears to be a manifestation of fear or discomfort, possibly associated with guilt or insecurity. The use of a negative directive or command ("Sumo, get in the shower you stink") suggests a sense of shame or unworthiness. The fear in the brown eyes of the dreamer indicates that he or she is aware of this negative attitude or perception. The use of fancy, expensive shampoo may symbolize an attempt to cover up or disguise the perceived shortcomings of the dreamer. The fact that the dreamer is carried down the stairs suggests a lack of autonomy or control, possibly due to feeling burdened or oppressed in waking life. Overall, the dream may reflect a desire for acceptance or approval from others, as well as a need to overcome feelings of inadequacy or inferiority.

Dory

2023

91. Dory

Dory designing from scratch. 3-D printed hull, made to measure small diving craft. Composite Air cylinders, moulded into the hull. Full tank below decks, enclosed wheelhouse and dive control. "Perfect, but too expensive," let's just build one, same as the last. Wasted dream.

Dream Interpretation

John's vision of designing and creating a small diving vessel with advanced features like 3-D printed hull, composite air cylinders, enclosed wheelhouse, and dive control represent the dreamer's desire to create something innovative and unique. The dreamer mentions that the design is too expensive, and they end up building the same as the last one, indicating a feeling of compromise and missed opportunity. The mention of the wasted dream suggests that the dreamer may feel like their desire to create something new and innovative is not being realized, and they are settling for less instead.

Overall, the dream may represent John's feeling of not being able to fully achieve their goals due to practical or financial constraints.

Knife

2023

92. Knife

Sat at the table, plate full of steak and eggs. Suddenly realised I'd forgotten my steak knife back in my room. Panic attack, what should I do? Rub my way through the steak or leave and fetch the Knife. It takes so long to find my room that I lose my way and the steak is lost.

Dream Interpretation

The dream could symbolize a lack of preparation or organization in the dreamer's waking life. The steak and eggs on the plate suggest a satisfying or abundant situation that the dreamer is currently enjoying. However, the missing steak knife represents an obstacle or challenge that the dreamer needs to overcome to fully enjoy this situation. The panic attack could signify anxiety or stress caused by uncertainty about how to deal with the challenge. The dreamer's indecision about whether to continue with the food or leave to fetch the knife could indicate a lack of clarity in decision-making. Losing the way and losing the steak could relate to the fear of losing or missing out on opportunities because of not being adequately prepared or organized.

Unreal

2023

93. Unreal

A world where I swim miles yet don't get wet.

Climb steep muddy banks but never reach the top.

Slide back down and get enveloped in carpet.

Sucked down into a floor finding myself breathing food fumes. Never getting or finding what I'm after. Always searching this unreal world.

Dream Interpretation

The dream may symbolize John's feelings of being unfulfilled in his search for a meaningful goal or purpose in life. The inability to get wet while swimming may represent a sense of detachment from one's emotions or a lack of depth in one's relationships. Climbing steep, muddy banks without reaching the top may indicate obstacles or challenges that prevent John from reaching his desired destination. Sliding back down and being enveloped in carpet may suggest feeling trapped or stuck in a cycle of frustration and disappointment. Being sucked down into a floor and breathing food fumes may symbolize feeling overwhelmed or suffocated by mundane or materialistic concerns. The overall theme of searching in an unreal world may suggest John's desire for something more meaningful or authentic in his life.